YOUR BIGFOOT EXPEDITION

YOUR BIGFOOT EXPEDITION

Timothy Wayne Williams

YOUR BIGFOOT EXPEDITION

ISBN: 979-8-9913175-0-4

Copyright © 2024 by Timothy Wayne Williams

All rights reserved.

Published in the United States
by Baldwin Brown Books
BaldwinBrownBooks.com

BALDWIN BROWN

Foreword

My journey into the realm of Timothy Wayne Williams' captivating Bigfoot paintings took place on social media, where his creations immediately left a lasting impression on me. The intricate details and powerful narratives woven into each piece spoke volumes, and I was certain that his art held the potential to bring immense joy and fascination to all who beheld it.

I shared my deep admiration for his work in a phone call, where I expressed the profound inspiration and joy it brought me. I knew his artistry had the power to engage audiences worldwide, so I invited him to show his work at my Cryptid Conference in the United Kingdom. Although he was unable to attend in person, we decided to bring in some of his paintings to call attention to his work.

In the following pages, you will embark on an enchanting exploration of the hidden world of Bigfoot art, guided by Timothy's incredible talent and vision. It is with great pleasure that I invite you to open your heart and mind to the beauty, mystery and sheer delight that his paintings offer. Prepare to be uplifted, inspired and enthralled by this incredibly talented artist, Timothy Wayne Williams.

— Daniel Lee Barnett
Bridgwater, Somerset, UK
July 2024

Introduction

The legend of Bigfoot, or Sasquatch, has long been debated. Is this creature real or imaginary? Is he science or myth?

In this book he is very real, and he is waiting to be found by you.

This is your yearlong expedition to spot and record your sightings of Bigfoot all over North America. This creature is everywhere in these locations.

You will start your expedition in the spring, searching, looking and counting the number of Bigfoot in each area. There's a spot for you to record how many of the creatures you see on each page. Sometimes they get brave and are easy to spot; other times they are very shy. They blend in with the background so well that they are almost impossible to see.

This expedition will take you along waterways Sasquatch are known to follow, deep into secluded forests, across remote farmland and to numerous other beautiful places. You never know where you'll see a Bigfoot. He may just show up at your campsite, so be prepared for anything!

Once you have made it through the book, go to the solutions pages in the back and see if you were right. You may have missed some.

So get ready for your journey, and keep your eyes open.

This is a test of your observation skills.

This is your cryptozoology mission.

This is your Bigfoot Expedition.

— *Timothy Wayne Williams*

Just a few suggestions:

Make sure you view the book in a well-lighted area. All of the Bigfoot should be visible to the naked eye, but if you are having difficulty finding them it may help to take a picture of the page and use zoom to get a closer look. An old-school magnifying glass would work well, too.

Enjoy your expedition.

SPRING

Your Bigfoot Expedition

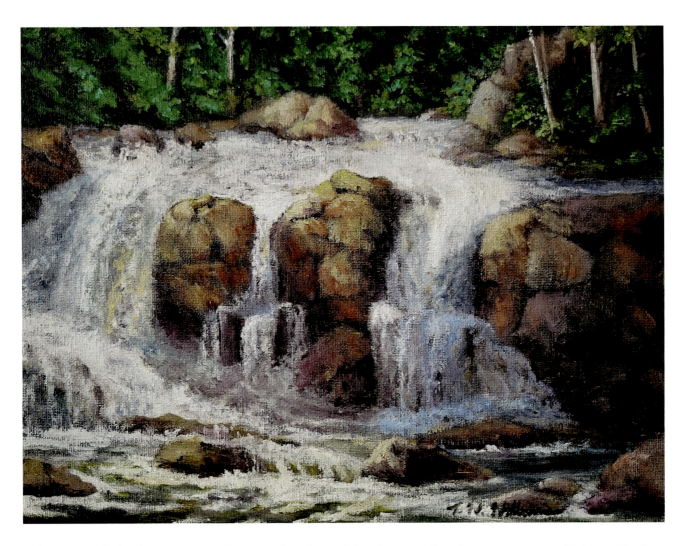

After careful planning and organization, it's time to begin your expedition. Today you start on a brisk late spring afternoon. There have been recent sightings in this area. Your job is to confirm the sightings and take an accounting of the creatures. Did you see any today?

CREATURE COUNT: _____

Spring

You find yourself looking over a beautiful mountain range. The vastness of the range makes you realize why it has been so hard for researchers to find these creatures.

CREATURE COUNT: _____

YOUR BIGFOOT EXPEDITION

Deep in the valley of the mountain range you spot a stone bridge. This is very unexpected in this remote area. Wonder how long it's been here, and who built it? Things worth pondering while you are traveling to your next location.

CREATURE COUNT: _____

Spring

After a long flight, drive and even longer hike, you find yourself in a different part of the country. You stop by an inviting stream. A sighting happened only a mile from here. The feeling of being watched is overwhelming.

CREATURE COUNT: _____

YOUR BIGFOOT EXPEDITION

As you move deeper into the forest, the shadows make it feel like a much later time of day. They are close. You can feel it.

CREATURE COUNT: _____

Spring

Hiking out a different way than you hiked in, you discover this hidden gem. You've been told this waterfall can be seen only in times of recent heavy rain. You are sure you aren't the only one who enjoys this view.

CREATURE COUNT: _____

Your Bigfoot Expedition

After a short visit back home to regroup and resupply, you find yourself in front of another waterway. The heavy overhang of the trees makes it feel like a cave.

CREATURE COUNT: _____

Spring

Exiting the tunnel of trees, you emerge into a lush valley full of color. You wish you could stay longer, but you have more places to see and record.

CREATURE COUNT: _____

YOUR BIGFOOT EXPEDITION

As the waning days of spring approach, you're now in Northern California. Hiking all day, you find yourself in the area where the famous Patterson/Gimlin footage was shot.

CREATURE COUNT: _____

Spring

This is the one place you couldn't wait to see on this expedition – Bluff Creek. What a great way to end spring, and this leg of your journey.

CREATURE COUNT: _____

SUMMER

YOUR BIGFOOT EXPEDITION

Spring is behind you now. This is the first hike into your latest research area. It's very warm but not intolerable. You stop to rest, watching the swaying tree tops and enjoying the light breeze.

CREATURE COUNT: _____

Summer

The next day, the sky has a strange look to it. Everything seems to be bathed in blue. A storm is coming. You quicken your pace, looking around you, ever vigilant.

CREATURE COUNT: _____

YOUR BIGFOOT EXPEDITION

After a rough night at camp, you head out. The storms kept you up late. You are sleepy and tired. The mountains are only about five miles away, and you see the valley unfold before you. Rumors have it that a family of Bigfoot live here.

CREATURE COUNT: _____

Summer

You roam around the base of the mountains for days. Completely by accident, you come across the most beautiful stream. It's so colorful in this light, and you think: "If I were a Bigfoot, this is where I would be."

CREATURE COUNT: _____

Time to head for home to regroup and resupply. After a couple weeks, you get an unexpected phone call: A researcher in Florida tells you of some really exciting encounters down that way. You scramble to amend your schedule. Within two days, you are on a plane touching down in Florida. Before long you are paddling a small boat among the cypress trees. The boat is a nice change from hiking.

CREATURE COUNT: _____

Summer

When the water gets too shallow, you go on foot. Trudging through the swamp with water to your knees, you notice how late it has gotten. Distracted by looking out for snakes, alligators and the possibility of a skunk ape sighting, you've lost all track of time. Need to return to camp fast.

CREATURE COUNT: _____

Your Bigfoot Expedition

The next morning, you pack up to leave. The path is easy to follow, even with the moss overgrowth.

CREATURE COUNT: _____

Summer

Leaving Florida in your rented SUV, you decide on a quick stop in Georgia. An older gentleman with a beautiful piece of land has been complaining about hearing screams from the woods when out in his rowboat.

CREATURE COUNT: _____

YOUR BIGFOOT EXPEDITION

Still heading north, you stop to camp in a state park in Tennessee. Instead of going deep into the forest, you decide to stay on the park's marked paths for a while. People here have recently been chased out of the park by something.

CREATURE COUNT: _____

SUMMER

Moving onto a more rugged trail, you pass by this lovely stream.

CREATURE COUNT: _____

YOUR BIGFOOT EXPEDITION

As you follow the stream, you realize it's part of a river. You follow the river for an hour or two. The moon is so bright you didn't realize how late it was. This wasn't the plan, but you make camp by the river.

CREATURE COUNT: _____

SUMMER

Leaving the river feels unsafe, but you keep moving on. Soon you come to another inviting stream. This is a good time to refill your canteens and rest in the cool water.

CREATURE COUNT: _____

The next day, you hear from a family that has a remote cabin. They have been having lots of problems. Their best way to get to civilization is by crossing a bridge next to their house. It seems that something has been destroying the bridge almost as fast as they can repair it. As you arrive at the property, you immediately see the damaged bridge. What could do that? Tomorrow you leave this part of the country. There's not a lot of time to investigate, but you do your best to validate the claims of the family.

CREATURE COUNT: _____

Summer

Your plan all along has been to get to the Pacific Northwest before fall. On a hot summer night you take the long flight to the West Coast. You were here in the spring, but a tip about the Bigfoot migration patterns brings you back for another look. You're told to check the coastal areas closely. Apparently some Bigfoot like to dig up clams for their sustenance. Hiking through the tall trees to the coast takes a lot of effort. In the distance, you can hear the ocean.

CREATURE COUNT: _____

YOUR BIGFOOT EXPEDITION

Finally you leave the lush forest and find the coastline. It's breathtaking and you have to remind yourself to do your job and document. Many Bigfoot have been seen in this area.

CREATURE COUNT: _____

Summer

Scrambling down to the shoreline, you see the beautiful untouched sand. You take off your shoes and feel the coolness of the sand between your toes. Not a bad way to end your day. The next morning, you pack up. The coast has so many things to see that you can't wait to get started.

CREATURE COUNT: _____

This part of the coast is gorgeous. The little coves and inlets hold so many surprises. You spend the day walking up and down beaches. Some cove areas are so calm they seem more like the banks of a big lake. It's difficult to focus on your search.

CREATURE COUNT: _____

SUMMER

You find the perfect place to end your long summer campaign. The mountains have opened up to a stunningly calm shoreline. You decide to make camp and are rewarded with the biggest, brightest full moon you have ever seen. It's so bright that you wonder if Bigfoot can be spotted by moonlight alone.

CREATURE COUNT: _____

AUTUMN

YOUR BIGFOOT EXPEDITION

The Midwest has some amazing hot spots of activity. You begin the fall leg of your expedition in Ohio. There are so many streams, creeks and rivers to explore. After an early start, you come upon this little stream. You get a strange feeling about this place – that overwhelming feeling of being watched.

CREATURE COUNT: _____

Autumn

The haze has started to lift now. This bridge has had many sightings by people crossing it.

CREATURE COUNT: _____

Farther into the wood, you find a perfect fall path. Daylight is fading though, so you can't linger too long.

CREATURE COUNT: _____

Autumn

Because you got back to the campsite so late, you have to get the fire going before you can set up your tent. The fire always makes you feel a little safer.

CREATURE COUNT: _____

The next morning you set off again. A hazy little creek seems like a good place to stop and search.

CREATURE COUNT: _____

Autumn

After a few hours you come across this small but beautiful waterfall. You are tempted to stick your feet into it. It's fall, but it's one of those hot Midwestern fall days.

CREATURE COUNT: _____

YOUR BIGFOOT EXPEDITION

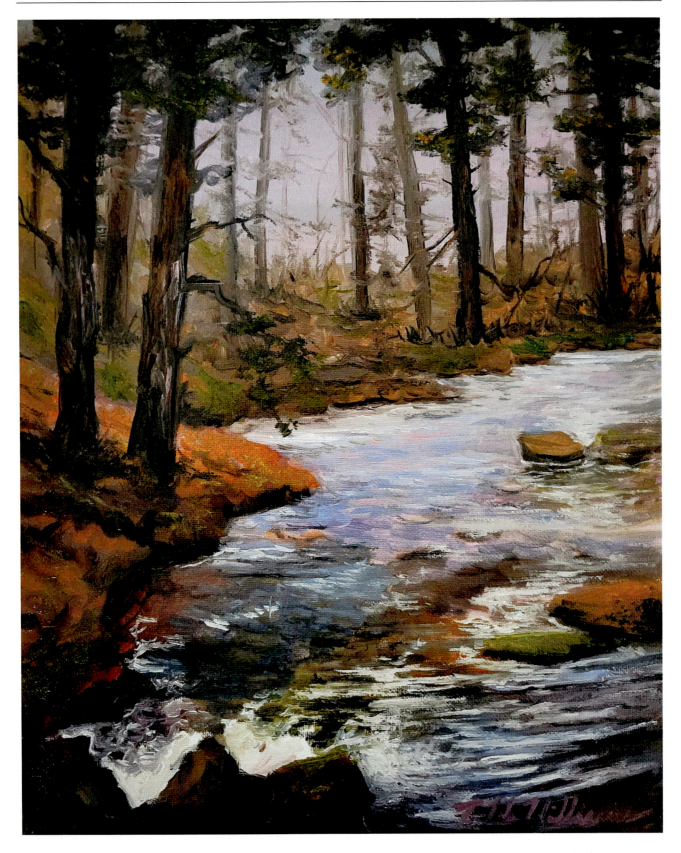

Heading into Southern Indiana, you continue your search. Indiana isn't known to have a lot of Bigfoot sightings, except for a couple areas down in this part of the state. Maybe you will get lucky today.

CREATURE COUNT: _____

Autumn

Another great stream to follow. You always seem to have good luck around streams. You can definitely confirm the Bigfoot stay close to waterways.

CREATURE COUNT: _____

Your Bigfoot Expedition

The waning sun seems to burn through the trees as you hike out. You and everything else are bathed in orange light. Might be tricky to see anything.

CREATURE COUNT: _____

Autumn

Another relaxing campfire. This is what makes autumn your favorite time to research. The warmth of the fire holds off the chill in the air. Wonder if anything is enjoying this fire from afar.

CREATURE COUNT: _____

Your Bigfoot Expedition

The following morning, it's slow going. Staying near the waterway is becoming increasingly difficult. The boulders covered in moss are slick and dangerous. Might not be the only dangerous thing here.

CREATURE COUNT: _____

Autumn

CREATURE COUNT: _____

Finally the going gets a little easier. You haven't seen any signs of civilization in days, until you see a lonely damaged boat. Too bad it doesn't still float. You could use a break from the hiking.

CREATURE COUNT: _____

Your Midwest trek is at an end. Time to go home, rest and resupply. Before you go, though, this beautiful stream and all its gorgeous colors invite you to rest awhile.

CREATURE COUNT: _____

Autumn

It's late fall now. You decide to head out West again. Some researchers claim Bigfoot migrate this way at fall's end. After yet another long flight, you reward yourself by checking into a stunning mountain hotel. Recently some guests claimed to have heard knocking on their windows at night. Seems strange for them to be this close, but it's worth checking out. You climb up high to get a good overview of the grounds.

CREATURE COUNT: _____

Your Bigfoot Expedition

Hiking into the mountains you get a little lost. Even though this waterfall is lovely, it's not on the map. You have a pretty good idea you are heading in the right direction, but there is a small worry in the back of your mind. You weren't planning on spending the night in the woods. You keep going.

CREATURE COUNT: _____

As the light fades, the landscape takes on a creepier vibe. The trees look scary. You finally realize where you are. You feel lucky there was at least some light left as you come out of the woods. Not the way you wanted to end your autumn exploration. As you see the hotel in the distance, you vow to not let that happen again. The hiking in winter is less forgiving.

CREATURE COUNT: _____

WINTER

Still out West. Winter has come in fast and furious. You were hoping to be out of the treacherous mountains by now, but there are a couple more areas to investigate. Locals claim to have seen Bigfoot around this pond.

CREATURE COUNT: _____

Winter

At night, you check out the other side of the pond. You're hoping the moon's glow will reveal some footprints.

CREATURE COUNT: _____

YOUR BIGFOOT EXPEDITION

At last! You see some prints. They seem to stop in this area. They must be close, very close.

CREATURE COUNT: _____

Winter

Continuing on this trail, you feel the quiet of the forest. Everything is silent. All that can be heard is the crunching of the snow under your feet. Eerie.

CREATURE COUNT: _____

In the distance you can see the warmth of the setting sun. It seems to be beckoning you forward. This forest is gorgeous. It's going to be hard to leave, but you must keep going. East is where you are headed. Need to find some flatter land to explore.

CREATURE COUNT: _____

Winter

Finally, some easier trails. The snow isn't nearly as deep as at your last location.

CREATURE COUNT: _____

YOUR BIGFOOT EXPEDITION

The sky is amazing here. Almost no light pollution. It's incredible. You feel so lucky to witness this. Hard to concentrate on what you've come to do.

CREATURE COUNT: _____

Winter

As the hours come and go, the sky changes. Its reflection seems to become one with the creek. Amazing to see.

CREATURE COUNT: _____

The next morning you take a new trail. It feels like a white tunnel. It's incredibly cold, but you don't mind. Maybe you will have some luck here.

CREATURE COUNT: _____

Winter

The trail seems to have led to the fence of an old farm. Bigfoot are known to hang around old farms. Need to check this area closely.

CREATURE COUNT: _____

YOUR BIGFOOT EXPEDITION

This place seems to be abandoned. Maybe the Bigfoot in the area think it's theirs now.

CREATURE COUNT: _____

Winter

On the opposite side of the property, you find an even older barn. You wonder if it would be safe to go in. More importantly, you wonder why the people left. Chased off, perhaps?

CREATURE COUNT: _____

Following the creek next to the old farm, you keep your head up. You heard something move through the woods.

CREATURE COUNT: _____

Winter

The noise seems to be moving now. Are there two? You follow along a bit farther but you don't want to lose the trail.

CREATURE COUNT: _____

YOUR BIGFOOT EXPEDITION

You would like to stay, but it's getting dark and much colder. You find the path back to camp and set off. It feels almost as if you are being followed, almost like being escorted out. Very unnerving.

CREATURE COUNT: _____

Winter

After some time at home to relax and unthaw yourself, it's time to hit the road again. Heading in an eastern direction again, you stop at a park that is famous for its Bigfoot activity. You aren't on the trail long before you see footprints. Very large footprints. They seem to have just been made!

CREATURE COUNT: _____

Your Bigfoot Expedition

You don't spot any more creatures for a couple of days, so you decide to keep moving. A river in the next state has had its share of sightings, some very recent. Getting to the river just before sunset was a blessing. There's still just enough light to do some searching.

CREATURE COUNT: _____

Winter

Deciding to stay another night, you're rewarded with this otherworldly moon. The next morning, you set off again.

CREATURE COUNT: _____

This was one location you made sure was part of the expedition – Northern Michigan to see the Northern Lights. You asked around to find the best place to see the lights and possibly Bigfoot.

CREATURE COUNT: _____

Winter

Heading east still, your expedition is almost over. You need to make the most of it. This forest has many Bigfoot legends. If you are very respectful, the Native Americans in the area might share some of their knowledge. The trail is rugged and the snow is back with a vengeance, but you think it will be worth it.

CREATURE COUNT: _____

YOUR BIGFOOT EXPEDITION

After nearly a full year and thousands of miles, you've reached the northeastern coast of the country in Maine. Unbelievably, you spot a Bigfoot right away! You wonder if there could be more though. It will be sad to go home, but you have done important research. You have taken an accounting of the number of Bigfoot across the nation. Your instincts are sharper, you powers of observation keener. You hope you can put together another expedition next year.

CREATURE COUNT: _____

Artist's Note

I sincerely hope you have enjoyed this book, and I thank you for spending some time on this expedition. Many long hours went into creating these paintings.

While this was my first attempt at something like this, by the Grace of God and your support, I hope it will be just the beginning.

About the Artist

Timothy is an artist, musician and writer living in Indianapolis. His paintings can be seen in public and private collections all over the world.

Contact:

twwilliamsfinearts@yahoo.com

Facebook: T.W. Williams Fine Arts

Instagram: Timothy_Wayne_Williams_

X: @TWWilliamsart

CREATURE COUNTS

Creature Counts

Page 10

Page 11

Page 12

Page 13

Page 14

Page 15

Page 16

Page 17

Page 18

Your Bigfoot Expedition

Page 19

Page 22

Page 23

Page 24

Page 25

Page 26

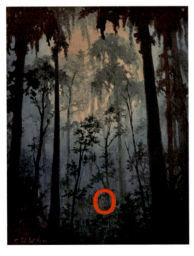

Page 27

Page 28

Page 29

Creature Counts

Page 30

Page 31

Page 32

Page 33

Page 34

Page 35

Page 36

Page 37

Page 38

Your Bigfoot Expedition

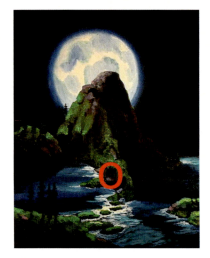

Page 39

Page 42

Page 43

Page 44

Page 45

Page 46

Page 47

Page 48

Page 49

Creature Counts

Page 50

Page 51

Page 52

Page 53

Page 54

Page 55

Page 56

Page 57

Page 60

Your Bigfoot Expedition

Page 61

Page 62

Page 63

Page 64

Page 65

Page 66

Page 67

Page 68

Page 69

Creature Counts

Page 70

Page 71

Page 72

Page 73

Page 74

Page 75

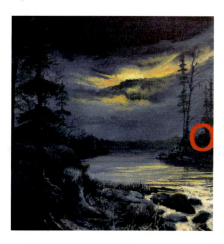

Page 76

Page 77

Page 78

Page 79

Page 80

Made in the USA
Las Vegas, NV
25 September 2024

fe753ecc-2c29-44e1-a7cc-c71d2dc4d983R01